West Virginia

BY ANN HEINRICHS

Content Adviser: Paul Rakes, Assistant Professor of History, West Virginia University
of Technology, Montgomery, West Virginia

Reading Adviser: Dr. Linda D. Labbo, Department of Reading Education,
College of Education, The University of Georgia

COMPASS POINT BOOKS MINNEAPOLIS, MINNESOTA

Compass Point Books
3109 West 50th Street, #115
Minneapolis, MN 55410

Visit Compass Point Books on the Internet at *www.compasspointbooks.com*
or e-mail your request to *custserv@compasspointbooks.com*

On the cover: Falls in Blackwater Falls State Park

Photographs ©: Corbis/David Muench, cover, 1; PhotoDisc, 3, 5, 44 (bottom); Robert McCaw, 7, 25, 44 (middle); Index Stock Imagery/Martin Fox, 8; Thomas Fletcher, 9; Unicorn Stock Photos/ChromoSohm/Sohm, 11, 24; Stock Montage Inc., 12; North Wind Picture Archives, 13, 16, 31; Hulton/Archive by Getty Images, 14, 15, 17, 18, 19, 35, 41, 46; U.S. Department of Agriculture/ARS Photo Library, 20, 42; Unicorn Stock Photos/Andre Jenny, 21; John Elk III, 23; Link/Visuals Unlimited, 26; Courtesy of West Virginia Division of Tourism/Steve Shaluta, 27, 43 (top); Pat Anderson/Visuals Unlimited, 28; Marc Epstein/Visuals Unlimited, 29; Courtesy of West Virginia Division of Tourism, 32, 33; Courtesy of West Virginia Division of Tourism/David Fattaloh, 34, 39, 47, 40 (top); Corbis/Richard T. Nowitz, 36; Mark E. Gibson/Visuals Unlimited, 37 (top); Courtesy of West Virginia Corps of Engineers, 37 (bottom), 45; Photo Network/Bill Terry, 40; Robesus, Inc., 43 (state flag); One Mile Up, Inc., 43 (state seal); Robert Lyons/Visuals Unlimited, 44 (top).

Editors: E. Russell Primm, Emily J. Dolbear, and Christianne C. Jones
Photo Researcher: Marcie C. Spence
Photo Selector: Linda S. Koutris
Designer: The Design Lab
Cartographer: XNR Productions, Inc.

Library of Congress Cataloging-in-Publication Data
Heinrichs, Ann.
  West Virginia / by Ann Heinrichs.
      p. cm. — (This land is your land)
Includes bibliographical references (p.) and index.
ISBN 0-7565-0351-5 (hardcover : alk. paper)
 1. West Virginia—Juvenile literature. [1. West Virginia.] I. Title. II. Series.
 F241.3.H45 2004
  975.4—dc21   2002155730

Table of Contents

NOTE: In this book, words that are defined in the glossary are in **bold** *the first time they appear in the text.*

Welcome to West Virginia!

Archie George worked in the mines of West Virginia in the early 1900s. "I made eight dollars and one penny a day drivin' a mule in [those] mines," Archie said. "That was hard work."

Coal mining was West Virginia's major **industry** for many years. Thousands of people like Archie spent their lives in the mines. West Virginians still mine coal and now drill for oil and natural gas, too. Chemicals, steel, and glass are also produced in the state.

Because several rugged mountains cover most of the state, West Virginia's nickname is the Mountain State. People in these mountains and other parts of West Virginia have always valued their freedom. Their state motto is *Montani Semper Liberi,* which is Latin for "Mountaineers are Always Free."

West Virginia was once part of the state of Virginia. That changed when the Civil War (1861–1865) began. West Virginians broke away and formed their own state.

Now let's explore West Virginia. You'll be sure to enjoy the scenic beauty and rich history of the Mountain State.

▲ A mill in West Virginia's mountains

West Virginia's name tells exactly where it is—west of Virginia! West Virginia was part of Virginia, but it broke away in 1861.

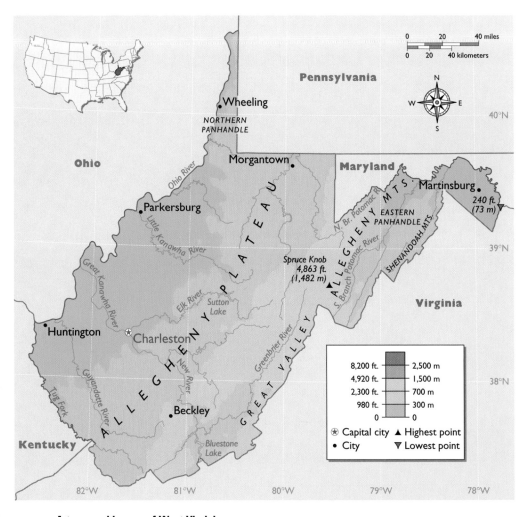

▲ **A topographic map of West Virginia**

West Virginia is a small state. Only nine other states are smaller. It's shaped like a frog, with its two back legs pointing north and east. Those "legs" are often called the Northern Panhandle and the Eastern Panhandle.

Pennsylvania and Maryland lie north of West Virginia. Ohio is to the northwest, and Kentucky is to the southwest. Virginia is to the south and east.

West Virginia lives up to its nickname—the Mountain State. It has the highest average height of any state east of the Mississippi River. Viewed from the air, West Virginia looks rugged and wild. Forests cover most of the state and are home to deer, bears, foxes, opossums, and raccoons.

▲ Foxes live in West Virginia's forests.

▲ **The Appalachian Mountains run through West Virginia.**

West Virginia lies within the Appalachian Mountain range. Two major sections of the Appalachians are in West Virginia. The Great Valley region runs along the eastern edge of the state. The Allegheny **Plateau** covers the rest of West Virginia.

The Great Valley is named for its chain of river valleys. This area is often called the Appalachian Ridge and Valley region. Rivers cut through the mountains in a northeast-to-southwest direction. The rich soil in these valleys is great for farming. The Blue Ridge Mountains are on the tip of the Eastern Panhandle.

▲ A covered bridge in Walkersville, which is located in central West Virginia

The Allegheny Plateau is often called the Appalachian Plateau. Several rivers and streams wind through its rugged hills. The biggest cities lie in the river valleys of the Allegheny Plateau. Southern and central West Virginia contain the state's richest coal deposits. The eastern part of the plateau rises up to the Allegheny Mountains, where West Virginia's highest peaks are located.

A natural dividing line separates the Great Valley and the Allegheny Plateau. This steep "wall" of mountains is called the Allegheny Front. Waters west of the Allegheny Front end up in the Gulf of Mexico. Those to the east flow toward the Atlantic Ocean.

The Ohio River forms much of West Virginia's northwest border. It's a major tributary, or branch, of the Mississippi River. Many rivers in western West Virginia flow into the Ohio River. One is the Great Kanawha River. Charleston, the state capital and largest city, lies along the Great Kanawha. The Potomac River borders part of the Eastern Panhandle.

West Virginia is hot in summer and cool in winter. The northern mountains get the most rain and snow. In the spring, melting snow causes the rivers to flood. Dams on the rivers help protect West Virginia towns when this happens. During the Buffalo Creek flood of 1972, however, a dam failed. More than one hundred people died as water rushed over their homes.

▲ The Potomac River flows along part of the Eastern Panhandle.

Two thousand years ago, Mound Builders lived in West Virginia. They built enormous mounds that they used as burial sites. Many of these mounds still remain near Charleston and Moundsville.

Later, many Native American groups built villages in

▲ A Native American village from the late 1500s located in what is present-day West Virginia

West Virginia. The mountains and valleys made excellent hunting grounds. However, this caused problems among the different Native American groups hunting in the same area. The Iroquois pushed other groups west and gained control of most of what is now West Virginia. The Delaware and Shawnee still sometimes hunted in West

▲ English colonists claimed part of present-day West Virginia after they arrived in 1607.

Virginia even after they had moved to Ohio. Some of the hunting trails created by these groups would later become major roads.

England established its Virginia **Colony** in 1607. Virginia **colonists** also claimed lands west of the Allegheny Mountains. These lands included what is now West Virginia. In 1727, German settlers moved in from Pennsylvania. They established New Mecklenburg, which is present-day Shepherdstown.

▲ Native Americans and colonists just before a conflict on the Ohio River during the 1700s

During the French and Indian War (1754–1763), Native Americans joined French troops in fighting for the region. The French were defeated. However, the Native Americans kept fighting to keep their lands. Finally, they were forced to leave and more settlers rushed in. Soon after this, Virginia and the other colonies fought the Revolutionary War (1775–1783). The colonists won, and the United States of America was created.

Virginians east and west of the Alleghenies had many

differences. Their lifestyles and viewpoints often clashed. People in the west were fiercely independent. They had small farms in the hills and valleys. They built factories and mills along the rivers. They also mined coal, salt, natural gas, and other minerals.

Many eastern Virginians owned **plantations.** They used African slaves for labor. Easterners were usually wealthier. The state's laws often favored people in the east.

▲ Slaves prepare to journey south to meet their new owners after a sale in Richmond, Virginia, during the mid-1800s.

▲ A slave woman holds her child up for John Brown to see as he is led away to be hanged in 1859.

In 1859, John Brown led a raid at Harpers Ferry. This historic spot is located on the far-eastern border of present-day West Virginia. Brown was an abolitionist, which is someone who wanted to end slavery. He took over an arsenal, or weapons storehouse. Brown meant to arm slaves for an uprising, but he was caught and hanged.

Soon Northern and Southern states split apart over the issue of slavery. The two sides fought the Civil War. Virginia joined the South, or Confederate, side. The state's western counties, however, did not want to join the other Southern states. In 1861, they voted to stay with the North, or the Union. Later that year,

▲ **Civil War soldiers near Harpers Ferry in 1864**

the Civil War's first land battle took place at Philippi, which is located in present-day West Virginia. In 1863, Virginia's western counties became the separate state of West Virginia.

After the war, West Virginia's industries grew. New factories made glass, steel, and chemicals. Coal mining, however, was the state's biggest industry. During the early 1900s, most West Virginians worked in the coal mines.

▲ John L. Lewis was the president of the United Mine Workers of America from 1920 until 1960.

Mining was a hard life, and it was dangerous work. Miners worked long hours underground. Explosions and other accidents killed hundreds of miners. Many also developed black lung disease. Miners sometimes joined groups such as the United Mine Workers **union** to fight for safer working conditions and higher wages. In West Virginia, coal wars were fought over attempts to form unions, and some miners were even killed. The coal companies did not want their miners to join unions.

Unions did not really take hold in West Virginia until the 1930s. This was when the Great Depression swept across the country. Economic hardship left millions out of work. Many of West Virginia's factories and mines closed. They finally opened

▲ Unemployed miners in Jere Scotts Run collect relief money during the Great Depression.

again during World War II (1939–1945). The state's steel and chemicals were much-needed war supplies.

West Virginia's coal industry went up and down like a yo-yo. The nation's need for coal dropped in the 1950s. New machines took the place of miners. Thousands of people left the state. Many who remained were unemployed. In the 1970s, coal was again in demand. During the 1980s, however, it declined once more.

▲ **A man collects water samples at Morgan's Spring to check for pollution.**

Today, state leaders are working hard to attract new industries. They know it's dangerous to depend on coal. Now, most workers have jobs in services or trades. West Virginia is also trying to protect its forests and other natural areas.

Government by the People

Charleston is West Virginia's capital city. Nine different types of marble were used to create the capitol building there. A glistening golden dome sits on top of the capitol.

▲ The state capitol in Charleston

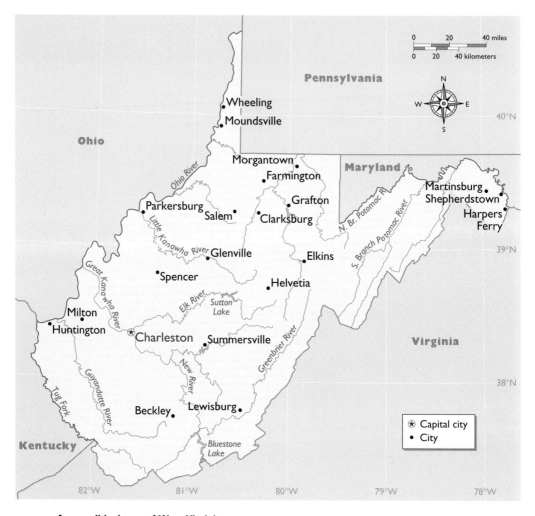

▲ **A geopolitical map of West Virginia**

West Virginia's state government works much like
the national government. It's divided into three branches—
legislative, executive, and judicial. This is called the checks
and balances system. The three branches check on one
another to balance the governing power. Each branch keeps

the others from becoming too powerful.

The legislative branch makes the state laws. It also decides how the state will spend its money. Voters elect lawmakers to serve in the state legislature. It has two houses, or parts. One is the 34-member senate. The other is the 100-member house of delegates.

The executive branch carries out the state's laws. West Virginia's governor is the head of the executive branch. Voters choose a governor every four years. The governor may serve only two terms in a row.

▲ State senators meet in this room in the state capitol in Charleston.

The voters also elect five other executive officers.

The judicial branch is made up of several different levels of courts. Judges on these courts listen to cases. They hear arguments for and against people who are accused of breaking the law. Then a jury decides whether the person is guilty or not guilty. West Virginia's highest court is the supreme court of appeals. Its five judges are elected to twelve-year terms.

West Virginia is divided into fifty-five counties. Voters in each county elect a circuit clerk, a county clerk, and county commissioners. Most cities and towns also elect

▲ The Jefferson County Courthouse was rebuilt in 1836. Judges still decide cases there today.

a mayor or manager and a city council.

It may seem that only adults can affect their government. After all, only adults can register to vote. However, West Virginia has called upon children to vote several times. Students around the state were asked to vote for the state bird, the state flower, and the state tree. They elected the cardinal, the rhododendron, and the sugar maple. State lawmakers then voted the students' wishes into law.

▲ Children in West Virginia chose the cardinal as their state bird.

Coal is still the state's greatest natural resource. Coal deposits lie beneath about two-thirds of the state. These deposits are made of bituminous, or soft, coal. The heaviest coal mining takes place in the southern counties.

Certain types of West Virginia coal give off little sulfur when burned. They are in high demand because they cause less air pollution.

The western part of the state also contains petroleum, which is an oil, and natural gas. Salt, limestone, and sand are mined in West Virginia, too. Some of the sand is used to make glass.

Chemicals are West Virginia's leading factory products. Most of these chemicals are

▲ One of West Virginia's mines

made from mining products—coal, oil, gas, and salt. Chemicals such as plastic and medicine are also made in West Virginia. Some of the state's factories make steel, tin, and other metals. In turn, these metals are used for hardware, including plumbing pipes and tools. Other factories make parts for cars and spacecraft.

Much glassware and pottery come from West Virginia. Craftspeople make

▲ A West Virginian making a glass bowl

drinking glasses, bottles, and stained glass. The state's rich clay deposits are made into dishes, bricks, and tiles.

West Virginia's most valuable farm products are chickens and eggs. Beef and dairy cattle are important, too. Dairy cows produce milk that is used for several dairy products made in

▲ Cattle graze on a pasture in front of a barn in Marlinton.

West Virginia. Sheep, hogs, pigs, and turkeys are other valuable farm animals. Sheep farmers shear the sheep for their wool. Some farmers keep bees for their honey. Others raise trout on "fish farms."

West Virginia is one of the nation's top apple-growing states. In fact, West Virginians were the first to grow Golden

Delicious and Grimes Golden apples. The Golden Delicious apple is the state fruit. Peaches are another delicious West Virginia fruit.

Hay is the state's leading field crop, followed by corn and tobacco. Farmers use most of their hay, corn, and oats as animal feed. Many farmers also grow soybeans and wheat.

▲ Apples growing in an orchard in Charleston

Service industries now employ the most people in the state. Service industries provide services rather than products. They include food stores, schools, hospitals, and gas stations. People who drive trucks, program computers, and work at tourist sites are all service workers. Medical professionals who care for the sick and the elderly are service workers. They use their skills to make life easier for others.

West Virginia's **pioneers** had roots in Scotland, England, and Germany. Many of them lived in the mountains, far from cities and towns. They kept the customs, arts, and speech of their homelands. They also took great pride in being independent. As the state motto says, "Mountaineers Are Always Free"!

Mountain communities had a **culture** of their own. They had names for every ridge, gap, **holler,** and fork in the road. In the forests, they picked greens and berries and dug for ginseng roots. They often gathered for quilt making, fiddling, and community dinners.

Today, almost two out of every three West Virginians still live in rural areas. Those are regions outside of cities and towns. The capital, Charleston, is the largest city. Next in size are Huntington, Parkersburg, and Wheeling. All three lie along the Ohio River.

West Virginia had 1,808,344 residents in 2000. That made it thirty-seventh in population among all the states. About 95 out of 100 West Virginians are white. This group includes

▲ **Weaving was a tradition and a craft of the Appalachian people.**

descendants of Italian, Polish, and other European **immigrants.** Others residents are African-American, Asian, and Native American.

Folk music is a proud **tradition** in West Virginia. Mountain folks handed down songs and fiddle tunes for many generations. Charleston's Vandalia Gathering celebrates

People come together on the grounds of the state capitol during the Vandalia Gathering.

32

mountain culture with musicians, dancers, and storytellers. Musicians play folk music on their fiddles, banjos, mandolins, and guitars. Some people come to dance. They enjoy traditional Irish, Scottish, Swiss, Croatian, and Appalachian dances.

Glenville holds the West Virginia State Folk Festival every year. Summersville hosts the Bluegrass Country Music Festival. The Appalachian Heritage Festival is in Shepherdstown. It's a weeklong celebration of mountain music, dance, and arts.

▲ Antique cars are featured in the Lion's Club parade during the State Folk Festival in Glenville.

Many **ethnic** groups hold festivals, too. Helvetia's
Community Fair celebrates German and Swiss cultures.
Clarksburg holds an Italian Heritage Festival. Some festivals
celebrate favorite crops and foods. They include Milton's
Pumpkin Festival, Salem's Apple Butter Festival, and
Spencer's Black Walnut Festival.

The third Saturday in October is Bridge Day. It's held
at the New River Gorge Bridge in Fayette County. The biggest

▲ **Parachuters at the New River Gorge Bridge on Bridge Day**

attractions are "daredevil" events. People parachute and **rappel** off the bridge. The Mountain State Forest Festival takes place in Elkins. People compete in wood-chopping, log-stacking, and sawing contests. They enjoy plenty of local food and music, too.

West Virginia's mountains are great places for camping, hiking, and wildlife watching. Adventurous folks take river rides in kayaks and rafts. In the winter, skiing is popular.

West Virginia's most famous writer was Pearl

▲ Pearl Buck (in 1938) was a famous writer who came from West Virginia.

Buck. Her novel *The Good Earth* (1931) tells about Chinese peasants' lives. She won two great awards—the Pulitzer Prize and the Nobel Prize for literature.

Novelist John Knowles was a West Virginian, too. His best-known book is *A Separate Peace* (1959). Actors Joanne Dru and Don Knotts came from West Virginia. Gymnast Mary Lou Retton was also from West Virginia. She won a gold medal in the 1984 Olympic Games.

Just how deep and dark were West Virginia's old coal mines? Visit Beckley and see for yourself. Real miners take visitors deep into an underground mine. You'll see how mining was done in the "pick and shovel" days. Be sure to wear a jacket. It's chilly down there!

Rich mine owners had quite a different life. At Bramwell, you can tour some of their elegant homes. You'll see why Bramwell is called the Village of Millionaires.

You'll step back 2,000 years in time at Grave Creek Mound. It was built by Mound Builders called the Adena people. It's the largest cone-shaped Adena mound in America. Scientists

▲ A statue of a coal miner at Beckley shows what mining work was like.

figure it took more than 60,000 tons (54,420 metric tons) of earth to build it.

John Brown led his anti-slavery raid at Harpers Ferry. Today, the site explores the many historic events that took place there.

A young African-American named Booker T. Washington taught Sunday school at the African Methodist Church near Malden. Washington went on to found Alabama's Tuskegee Institute, a college for African-Americans.

Bulltown Historic Area in Burnsville is a Civil War battle site. There, you'll see

▲ Harpers Ferry was the site of John Brown's antislavery revolt.

▲ The McCauley Barn at the Bulltown Historic Area in Burnsville

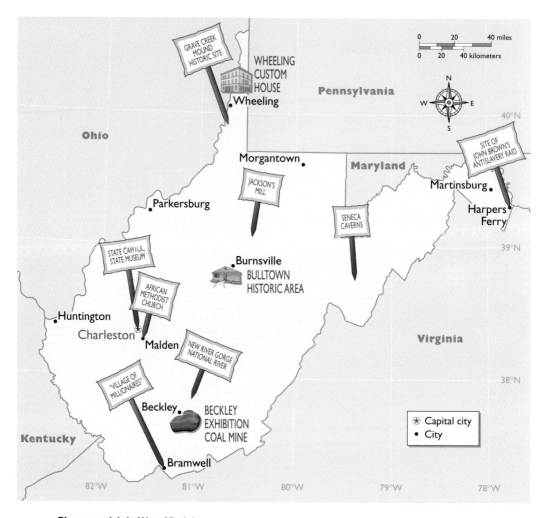

GRAVE CREEK MOUND HISTORIC SITE

WHEELING CUSTOM HOUSE

• Wheeling

Pennsylvania

Ohio

• Morgantown

JACKSON'S MILL

Maryland

• Parkersburg

Martinsburg •

SITE OF JOHN BROWN'S ANTISLAVERY RAID

Harpers• Ferry

SENECA CAVERNS

40°N

39°N

38°N

STATE CAPITOL, STATE MUSEUM

• Burnsville

BULLTOWN HISTORIC AREA

AFRICAN METHODIST CHURCH

• Huntington

Charleston ✵

• Malden

NEW RIVER GORGE NATIONAL RIVER

Virginia

"VILLAGE OF MILLIONAIRES"

Beckley •

BECKLEY EXHIBITION COAL MINE

✵ Capital city
• City

Kentucky

• Bramwell

82°W   81°W   80°W   79°W   78°W

0   20   40 miles
0   20   40 kilometers

N
W E
S

▲ **Places to visit in West Virginia**

battlefield trenches and soldiers' equipment. Jackson's Mill was Confederate general "Stonewall" Jackson's childhood home. Its buildings include a water-powered mill and a blacksmith shop. Craftspeople demonstrate their skills there, too.

The magnificent state capitol stands in Charleston. Its

glistening golden dome can be seen for miles around. Nearby is the State Museum. One of its exhibits explores the wreck of the slave ship *Henrietta Marie.*

Wheeling is often called the birthplace of West Virginia. That "birth" took place in the Wheeling Custom House. Delegates met there and decided to break away from Virginia. This decision led to West Virginia's statehood.

Where would you find dripstone, flowstone, gypsum flowers, and cave popcorn? They're all rock formations in Seneca Caverns. Seneca Indians once used these caves for

▲ **This rock formation at the Seneca Caverns is called the Bridal Chamber.**

▲ Mountains and forests surround the New River Gorge.

shelter and religious ceremonies. Tour the caves, and see how small you feel among their towering chambers.

The New River Gorge winds through deep canyons in southern West Virginia. Its bridge is the world's longest single-arch steel bridge. Take a hike through the surrounding forest. You'll see wildlife, waterfalls, and awesome views of the rushing river. West Virginia is a great place to explore!

Important Dates

1727 German settlers from Pennsylvania establish New Mecklenburg (present-day Shepherdstown).

1755 French and Indians defeat troops under Colonel George Washington and British General Edward Braddock.

1773 West Virginia's first permanent settlement is made in the Kanawha Valley.

1815 Natural gas is discovered near Charleston.

1836 West Virginia's first railroad reaches Harpers Ferry.

1859 John Brown leads a raid at Harpers Ferry.

1861 Western Virginia counties separate from Virginia and organize a government supporting the Union in the Civil War.

1863 President Abraham Lincoln declares West Virginia the thirty-fifth state on June 20.

1890 Two unions join forces to form the United Mine Workers union.

1907 The worst mine disaster in U.S. history occurs at mines in Monongah when 362 men and boys die.

1921 West Virginia becomes the first state to charge a sales tax.

1924 Democrat John W. Davis of Clarksburg runs for president; Republican Calvin Coolidge defeats him.

1954 The West Virginia Turnpike opens.

1968 Seventy-eight people die in a coal mine disaster in Farmington.

1972 The Buffalo Creek flood kills 125 people.

1988 West Virginian Robert C. Byrd becomes chairman of the U.S. Senate Appropriations Committee; he serves until 1995.

2002 A major flood in May causes more than $20 million in damage to southern West Virginia.

Glossary

colonists—people who settle a new land for their home country

colony—a territory that belongs to the country that settles it

culture—a group of people who share beliefs, customs, and a way of life

descendants—a person's children, grandchildren, great-grandchildren, and their offspring

ethnic—relating to a nationality or culture

holler—a low part of land, such as a small valley or basin; also known as a hollow

immigrants—people who leave their country to settle in another country

industry—a business or trade

plantations—large farms in the South, usually worked by slaves

plateau—high, flat land

pioneers—people who explore or settle in a new land

rappel—to lower oneself down with a rope

tradition—a custom that is common among a family or group

union—an organization of workers

Did You Know?

★ The dome on West Virginia's state capitol is 292 feet (89 meters) high. That's higher than the dome on the U.S. Capitol in Washington, D.C.

★ The chandelier in the state capitol's dome weighs about 4,000 pounds (1,814 kilograms). It has the lighting power of 15,000 candles!

★ The first Mother's Day was celebrated at Andrews Methodist Episcopal Church in Grafton on May 10, 1908.

★ Most glass marbles are made in the Parkersburg area.

★ The world's largest sycamore tree is in Webster Springs.

★ The first free rural mail delivery started in Charles Town in 1896.

★ Nearly three-fourths of West Virginia is covered by forests.

★ West Virginia was the first state to have a sales tax.

State capital: Charleston

State motto: *Montani Semper Liberi* (Latin for "Mountaineers Are Always Free")

State nickname: Mountain State

Statehood: June 20, 1863; thirty-fifth state

Land area: 24,087 square miles (62,385 sq km); **rank:** forty-first

Highest point: Spruce Knob, 4,863 feet (1,482 m) above sea level

Lowest point: 240 feet (73 m) above sea level along the Potomac River in Jefferson County

Highest recorded temperature: 112°F (44°C) at Martinsburg on July 10, 1936, and at Moorefield on August 4, 1930

Lowest recorded temperature: –37°F (–38°C) at Lewisburg on December 30, 1917

Average January temperature: 32°F (0°C)

Average July temperature: 72°F (22°C)

Population in 2000: 1,808,344; **rank:** thirty-seventh

Largest cities in 2000: Charleston (53,421), Huntington (51,475), Parkersburg (33,099), Wheeling (31,419)

Factory products: Chemicals, metal products, stone and clay products

Farm products: Chickens, beef cattle, turkeys, milk

Mining products: Coal, natural gas, petroleum

State flag: West Virginia's state flag shows the state coat of arms against a white background. Around the edges is a blue border. The coat of arms shows a miner and a farmer. They represent the state's mining and farming industries. Between them is a rock with the date of statehood—June 20, 1863. In front of the men are rifles. This means the people are willing to fight for their freedom. A banner at the top says "State of West Virginia." Below is a banner with the state motto. A wreath of rhododendron, the state flower, surrounds the coat of arms.

State seal: The state seal shows many of the symbols from the state coat of arms. At the bottom is the state motto. The back side of the seal shows several symbols of West Virginia's industry and natural areas.

State abbreviations: W.Va. (traditional); WV (postal)

State Symbols

State bird: Cardinal

State flower: Rhododendron

State tree: Sugar maple

State animal: Black bear

State fish: Brook trout

State butterfly: Monarch butterfly

State insect: Honeybee

State fruit: Golden Delicious apple

State gem: *Lithostrotiomella* (a fossil coral)

State soil: Monongahela silt loam

State colors: Old gold and blue

Making Golden Delicious Oatmeal

Golden Delicious apples are West Virginia's state fruit.

Makes two servings.

INGREDIENTS:

1 medium Golden Delicious apple

2/3 cup apple juice

2/3 cup water

1/8 teaspoon cinnamon

1/8 teaspoon nutmeg

2/3 cup quick-cooking oats

1/8 teaspoon salt

DIRECTIONS:

Make sure an adult helps you with the sharp knife and the hot stove. Peel and core the apple and chop it into small pieces. In a saucepan, mix the apple, juice, water, cinnamon, and nutmeg. Heat until it boils. Add the oats and salt. Cook 1 to 2 minutes, stirring enough to keep it from sticking to the bottom of the pan. Turn off the heat, and put a lid on the pan. Let it stand for a few minutes before serving.

West Virginia has three state songs. "The West Virginia Hills" (below) is the best known. The other two are "This Is My West Virginia" by Iris Bell and "West Virginia My Home" by Julian G. Hearne Jr.

"The West Virginia Hills"
Words by Ellen King, music by H. E. Engle

Oh, the West Virginia hills!
How majestic and how grand.
With their summits bathed in glory,
Like our Prince Immanuel's land!
Is it any wonder then,
That my heart with rapture thrills,
As I stand once more with loved ones
On these West Virginia hills?

O the hills, Beautiful hills,
How I love those West Virginia hills.
If o'er sea or land I roam
Still I think of happy home
And the friends among the West Virginia hills.

Pearl Buck (1892–1973) was a novelist. She is best known for *The Good Earth* (1931), for which she won a Pulitzer Prize. Buck (pictured above left) also won the 1938 Nobel Prize for literature. She was born in Hillsboro.

Phyllis Curtin (1922–) is an opera singer. She was born in Clarksburg.

Joanne Dru (1923–1996) was an actress. She starred with John Wayne in *Red River* and *She Wore a Yellow Ribbon.* Dru was born in Logan.

Don Knotts (1924–) is an actor. Knotts was born in Morgantown. He is best known for playing Barney Fife in television's *The Andy Griffith Show.*

John Knowles (1926–2001) was a novelist. His best-known work is *A Separate Peace* (1959). Knowles was born in Fairmont.

Peter Marshall (1927–) was the host of the original *Hollywood Squares* television show. He was born in Huntington.

Kathy Mattea (1959–) is a country music singer. She was born in Cross Lane.

Mary Lou Retton (1968–) is a gymnast. She was born in Fairmont. Retton won the gold medal for gymnastics in the 1984 Olympic Games. In 1997, she was inducted into the International Gymnastics Hall of Fame.

Walter Reuther (1907–1970) was a powerful labor leader. He was president of the United Auto Workers (UAW) and the Congress of Industrial Organizations (CIO). Reuther was born in Wheeling.

John D. Rockefeller IV (1937–) served as governor (1977–1985) and as a U.S. senator (1985–) from West Virginia. He was born in New York.

Eleanor Steber (1914–1990) was a concert and opera singer. She was born in Wheeling.

Cyrus Vance (1917–2002) was the U.S. secretary of state from 1977 to 1981. Vance was born in Clarksburg.

Booker T. Washington (1856–1915) founded Alabama's Tuskegee Institute (now Tuskegee University) for African-Americans. He was born in Virginia and grew up in West Virginia.

Harold Tucker Webster (1885–1952) was a cartoonist. He created "The Timid Soul" comic strip, with its meek character Casper Milquetoast. Webster was born in Parkersburg.

Chuck Yeager (1923–) is a retired Air Force test pilot and general. In 1947, he became the first human to break the sound barrier. That means he flew faster than the speed of sound. Yeager was born in Myra.

Want to Know More?

At the Library

Bial, Raymond. *Mist Over the Mountains: Appalachia and Its People.* New York: Houghton Mifflin, 1997.

Di Piazza, Domenica. *West Virginia.* Minneapolis: Lerner, 2002.

Faine, Edward Allan, and Joan C. Waites (illustrator). *Little Ned Stories.* Takoma Park, Md.: IM Press, 1999.

Fradin, Dennis Brindell. *West Virginia.* Danbury, Conn.: Children's Press, 1998.

Gray, Libba Moore, and Raúl Colón (illustrator). *My Mama Had a Dancing Heart.* New York: Orchard Books, 1995.

Joseph, Paul. *West Virginia.* Edina, Minn.: Abdo & Daughters, 1998.

Rylant, Cynthia, and Diane Goode (illustrator). *When I Was Young in the Mountains.* New York: Dutton, 1993.

On the Web

State of West Virginia
http://www.state.wv.us
To visit the state web site and learn about West Virginia's history, government, economy, and arts

West Virginia: Wild and Wonderful
http://www.callwva.com/index.htm
To learn about West Virginia's events, activities, and sights

Through the Mail

West Virginia Division of Tourism and Parks
2101 Washington Street East
Charleston, WV 25305
For information on travel and interesting sights in West Virginia

West Virginia Development Office
Capitol Complex
Building 6, Room 553
1900 Washington Street East
Charleston, WV 25305
For information on West Virginia's economy

On the Road

West Virginia State Capitol
1900 Kanawha Boulevard East
Charleston, WV 25305
304/558-3809
To visit West Virginia's state capitol

Index

About the Author

Ann Heinrichs grew up in Fort Smith, Arkansas, and lives in Chicago. She is the author of more than one hundred books for children and young adults on Asian, African, and U.S. history and culture. Ann has also written numerous newspaper, magazine, and encyclopedia articles. She is an award-winning martial artist, specializing in t'ai chi empty-hand and sword forms.

Ann has traveled widely throughout the United States, Africa, Asia, and the Middle East. In exploring each state for this series, she rediscovered the people, history, and resources that make this a great land, as well as the concerns we share with people around the world.